APOSTOLIC
MOMENTUM

Engaging The Marketplace

Dr. Frederick D. Acklin

Copyright © 2021 by Dr. Frederick D. Acklin. All rights reserved. No part of this publication may be reproduced, distributed, or transmitted in any form or by any means, including photocopying, recording, or other electronic or mechanical methods, without the prior written permission of the publisher, except in the case of brief quotations embodied in critical reviews and certain other noncommercial uses permitted by copyright law. For permission requests, write to the publisher, addressed "Attention: Permissions Coordinator," at the address below.

ISBN: 978-1-7372246-4-8

Publishing By: DemiCo National, LLC

www.DemiCoNational.com

TABLE OF CONTENTS

Forward By Bishop Kevin Foreman *(Page 7)*

1. Momentum (Page 9)
2. Overcome Opposition *(Page 18)*
3. Marketplace and Money *(Page 30)*
4. Exploits and Strategy *(Page 40)*
5. Tangible Results *(Page 47)*
6. Understanding Your Reign *(Page 59)*
7. Management *(Page 64)*
8. Mountains and Movements *(Page 69)*
9. Questionnaire & Practical Tips *(Page 73)*

FORWARD

Dr. Frederick Acklin is one of the rare modern voices that not only has the ability to not only teach the theory of apostolic momentum, but also demonstrate its power. In this book, which really reads like an instructional manual, Dr. Acklin lays out how one is to ascertain momentum in every movement in their life. The Bible teaches that we will be known by your fruit or what we produce. There is no purpose in our lives that transcends producing fruit. When we produce fruit, it is proof of our belief.

When we produce fruit, it is evidence of the existence of our great God. In this book, leaders and lay people alike will find themselves in the intricate tapestry which is life and be able to navigate to a place of momentum that allows them to see tangible results and maximize their outcomes. This is not just a book for

Christian leaders. This is a book for leaders who are Christians. That difference and distinction is important because often people will think that roles of prominence are only reserved for stages and people with microphones and platforms...not so. The reality is, it's for you.

Let's take this journey of Apostolic Momentum together. Apostolic simply deals with the foundational-transformational structure of everything that God did. The word apostle comes from the Greek work "apostello" which means, sent ones. Guess what? You and I were sent for a special mission. We were born for the times we are needed most, which is now. Let's do this thing together. Shalom

- Bishop Kevin Foreman

CHAPTER ONE
MOMENTUM

It has been said that all the world is a stage, if so then we are all laying our part and interconnectedly effecting others. We perceive that an unseen hand is holding all the strings and determining the outcomes of events. It seems as if some have an advantage or are favored to win, if this holds true then the characters could only have been predestined in their roles and outcomes. Whenever a character is created, there is always intention of productivity and an intended outcome.

The necessary functionality of the individual or thing must be programmed or allocated within the characters capacity. Hence, even a name is a descriptor of what the character usually will perform or accomplish. So, let's begin with an etymology of the world Apostolic and Momentum to understand the purpose of the momentum within the apostolic movement.

Apostolos

- *taken from the original word in the Greek (apostello, apostegazo o Apostereo, apostello.)*

- Definition: to order (one) to go to a place appointed. ("Apostello Meaning in Bible - New Testament Greek Lexicon ...") To send away, dismiss or to allow one to depart, that he may be in a state of liberty. To order one to depart, send off. To drive away apostolic means to function as a delegate on behalf of another.

In reference to the kingdom, Jesus sent out seventy men on an apostolic mission in Matthew 10 to go before Him as diplomat and to prepare the way. Likewise, today are to Apostolos and be sent out into the world to bring the kingdom of God upon the earth. Many have argued the necessity and biblical clarity of modern-day Apostles; however, we clearly see this pattern in Jesus. We later see it conducted with Apostle Paul in Acts 19.

- Acts 19- And when Paul had laid hands on them, the Holy Spirit came upon them, and they spoke with tongues and prophesied. Now the men were about twelve in all.

So, what we understand from the definition and passages that Jesus modeled is to spread the kingdom by imparting onto others and discipling them to make disciples. That's the biblical apostolic multiplication mission, those disciples are then sent out to further the kingdom expansion.

Next, lets look at the way or process by which the holy spirit enables the apostles to function by.

Momentum

- Definition: the strength or force that something has when it is moving; the strength or force that allows something to continue or to grow stronger or faster as time passes
- Synonyms: speed · pace · rate · tempo · impetus · swiftness ·

In physics momentum- is the product of the mass and velocity of an object It is a vector quantity, possessing a magnitude and a direction. If m is an object's mass and v is its velocity (also a vector quantity), then the object's momentum p is **p**=m**v**.[i]

When I look at these terms through the eyes of the spirit, I can see that mass (weight) and velocity (speed) can be redefined as the Mass=mantle of a person or mandate and velocity is the power released to bring the mandate to pass.

This book will further explain that an apostle on a mission must have both a commissioned mandate from God and the power released to execute the mandate.

Many today with the titles of Apostle can usually explain the mission they are called to accomplish however they lack the power to manifest results. This is where apostolic patterns must be trained and equipped in the full revelation of the five-fold mission of Christ. The bible explains that many are perishing due to lack of knowledge.

Paul, a great apostle of the faith, spoke about his entrance into the realm of power that was established by tribulation. What a contrast to the modern-day glorification and celebrity like lifestyle of modern-day apostleship.

- Acts 14:22- Confirming the souls of the disciples, and exhorting them to continue in the faith, and that we must through much tribulation enter into the kingdom of God.

The apostleship's fundamental workings allow for kingdom entrance, not just of the apostle's entrance, but of the entire body of Christ. Therefore, it would lend that the potency of the momentum is extracted and directly correlated to the direct charge and commission from Jesus Christ.

What do I mean by direct charge and commission? The magnitude of the mission of Jesus given directly to the Apostle must have the mass (weight) and (velocity) intensity to be established and bear fruit for centuries.

Mass-

- Definition: Capacity of force upon an object

Velocity-

- Definition: Speed at which force has expression and release.

Let me further explain this concept; the Kabod or weight of glory resting upon a man's mantle is related to the unlimited submission of a person's obedience to the Holy Spirit.

The Hebrew word kavod (K-V-D) has meant "importance", "weight", "deference", or "heaviness", but primarily kavod means "*glory*", "respect", "honor", and "majesty".

So, what is the Greek meaning for glory? doxa- glory. The honor, praise, and glory that comes from a good opinion. It's an appearance commanding respect, excellence, and magnificence. This term is used to describe God's nature and actions in self-manifestation.

Interestingly, the Hebrew word kabod, which is translated into English as "glory," has the root meaning of "weight" or "heaviness." This offers a clue that glory has to do with weight, and this is confirmed by passages such as 2 Corinthians 4:17, which speaks of the "weight of glory."

We can then conclude that measuring our apostolic momentum has to also factor in the weight/mass (kabod) resting upon the man in contrast to his velocity. In other words, many apostolic endeavors may seem to have slow velocity (expression) but once it begins it has great momentum. We start apostolic missions as pioneers usually, building from nothing into great masses of kingdom endeavors.

This then leaves our greatest component to the unseen worlds functioning being FAITH alone. Just like the speck or QUARK that has been named the smallest element of known existence.

Our Faith is the unseen force acting upon our apostolic endeavors. Trace this back to the brooding of the holy spirit.

Mature apostles do not just build churches. They build communities. Instead of people they build networks or companies of prophets and pastors.

CHAPTER TWO

OVERCOME OPPOSITION

Partnering with God is key to accomplishing anything that will outlast the rulership of the prince of this world. This is the way Jesus mastered His assignment, mandate and liberated humanity from becoming casualties of the system of the beast.

DOMINION IS ACCOMPLISHED THROUGH THRONES not Prayer. The church has misplaced the proper position of kingship with the priestly role that is limited to prayer and intercession. But Jesus said you shall reign with me, as Kings and Priests. We understand the priestly role very well, it is relational, easier to comprehend.

In contrast the kingship realm is almost unfathomable aspect of God to those who only embrace humans in the after the fall defeated place, outside of the garden. Jesus came restore all things and fulfill the original purpose of man *ie* His dominion upon the earth.

It is only from a realm of authorized RULERSHIP that one can reign in the earth and influence nations with the unstoppable DUNAMIS POWER of God.

So, what does kingship, thrones and rulership look like in the marketplace? It is the place of personal economy or the economics of your outputs and personal system of authority.

- Matthew 19:28 Jesus said to them, "Truly, I say to you, in the new world, when the Son of Man will sit on his glorious throne, you who have followed me will also sit on twelve thrones, judging the twelve tribes of Israel. Then Pharaoh said to Joseph, "Since God has made all this known to you, there is no one so discerning and wise as you. [40] You shall be in charge of my palace, and all my people are to submit to your orders. Only with respect to the throne will I be greater than you."

Discernment, Charge and Orders-

In the marketplace it shows up in our interactions with the world as discerning, wisdom, having charge or oversight and submission to our endeavors by peoples.

If we do a quick case study on the life of Joseph, from the scriptures we will see that he operated in dominion in the Egyptian hierarchy of Pharaoh. Joseph was able to overcome three types of opposition within his prophetic journey to destiny. Opposition from without, from within and spiritual wickedness in high places.

Joseph's first opposition was from his own family, which left him in a pit due to his dreaming and visions. He overcame by working his gifts regardless of the environment or circumstances. Pharaoh said he was discerning; he received this grace because he understood some opposition was his warrior training. The things that opposed him that were meant for his demise became his footstools of character formation and integrity. All of which catapulted him into the place of purpose and rulership.

Discernment allows us to understand things that are permanent conditions versus temporary incidents that can be overcome. Once we can discern the source of a predicament we can respond correctly. Had Joseph responded to the crisis of the famine with bitterness and indifference he would have missed his divine moment of elevation.

__Discernment-__

- Definition: the quality of being able to grasp and comprehend what is obscure: skill in discerning, acted wisely (1), cared (1), clever (1), consider (8), consider carefully (1), considers (1), diligently consider

Secondly, we will need to implore wisdom that instructs us into victory and success. Wisdom is principle in moving into apostolic momentum. Once you discern the opportunity, then wisdom allows one to fully engage with the appropriate response.

We also see the word wisdom. חכם (*hhakham*) is related to the idea of "separating," as this word means "one who is able to separate between what is good and bad." This one word can be translated as either "skill" when applied to a craftsman, or as "wise" when applied to a leader or counselor.

- Deuteronomy 1:13-Provide for yourselves wise (hhakham) men and understanding and knowing for your tribes and I will set them as rulers over you.

This scripture above implies that God sets those to rule over others must possess wisdom to be considered.

Charge-

This word really means rulership or responsibility to accomplish and desired outcome. Like we stated before the Apostleship is about having the authority to accomplish God's will upon earth. It is beyond just prophetically seeing the will of God, preparing people for the benefits but must hold the responsibility to bring it to pass.

Lastly, we must have people willing to submit to our orders. Every marketplace endeavor must have people that will support, be employed to, or aligned with the vision for functionality.

Failure to supply the team, company or ministry with clear orders will stop the productivity.

Submission to your orders is also how we operate legally and professionally. Once someone is placed in charge, they must have the ability to expect or rule over the people assigned to undergird or facilitate the operations.

- Romans 13:5 Therefore you must be subject, not only because of wrath but also for conscience' sake.

We must exercise our right to hire, maintain and give orders to workers (employees) that partner with the business in exchange for wages, rights, and benefits.

People are the greatest resource to our apostolic momentum and marketplace endeavors. We must excel in relational aspect of our dominion with tact, diplomacy, and integrity.

People management is so critical to effectiveness and the trajectory of our altitude and influence.

Here are a few tips for engaging and maintaining relationships that will maintain your rulership.

1. Encourage their personal development
2. Create psychological safety
3. Encourage teamwork and collaboration among employees
4. Recognize and reward your team for their hard work
5. Provide employees with tools and resources for success

6. Encourage creativity
7. Schedule regular one-on-one meetings[ii]

7 Mountains of Opposition Apostolic Leaders Must Overcome -

- Fear
- Confusion
- Discouragement
- Instability Emotional
- Arrogance and criticism
- Greed and lust
- Undisciplined, unrestricted living
- Laziness and sensual living
- Immorality and polluted living

HITTITES –

This name means terror. They were giants who brought fear, confusion, and discouragement to others. This is our enemy too because as spiritual Israelites we should only fear God and not anything other than God and not man. Proverbs 29:25 (NIV) says "Fear of man will prove to be a snare, but whoever trusts in the LORD is kept safe".

GIRGASHITES –

The meaning of the word "Girgashite" is as one who returns back from a pilgrimage. Therefore, they are people that go back and are earthly. They build their houses using clay which shows they are not stable in their mind-set. This is our enemy too because we have to be stable in our faith always based on Jesus Christ. In Isaiah 28:16 (ESV), "Thus says the Lord God, "Behold, I am the one who has laid as a foundation in Zion, a stone, a tested stone, a precious cornerstone, of a sure foundation: 'Whoever believes will not be in haste.'..."

AMORITES-

They were people who were arrogant and boastful in their speech, who were always challenging. They had high self-esteem and this pride led to finding fault in others. This is our enemy too because God is the only judge. So, if we judge others then we will also be arrogant before God. Proverbs 8:13 (NIV) says "To fear the LORD is to hate evil; I hate pride and arrogance, evil behavior and perverse speech."

CANAANITES-

This name means merchants who humiliate. They were financial giants. The Canaanites were motivated by greed and lust for the accumulation of earthly and material wealth. This is our enemy too as we cannot serve two masters and this world's possessions are temporary. James 4.4 (NIV) says "You adulterous people, don't you know that friendship with the world means enmity against God? Therefore, anyone who chooses to be a friend of the world becomes an enemy of God."

PERIZZITES-

They were people who had separated themselves and lived in unprotected, unwalled villages. They had no discipline and restrictions. This is our enemy because we have to completely surrender ourselves to God's commandments. Proverbs 25:28 (NIV) says "Like a city whose walls are broken through is a person who lacks self-control."

HIVITES-

They claimed to offer a good lifestyle, living by phrases such as "if it feels good do it", "don't worry what other people think" and "look out for number one". They lived a very luxurious life. This is our enemy because our spiritual life is a sacrificial one. 1 Tim.6.10 (NIV) says "for the love of money is a root of all kinds of evil. Some people, eager for money, have wandered from the faith and pierced themselves with many griefs."

JEBUSITES-

They were people who exploited and polluted others through immoral activities. This is our enemy because our body is a temple of our lord. Matthew 5:27-28 (NIV) says "You have heard that it was said, 'You shall not commit adultery.' But I tell you that anyone who looks at a woman lustfully has already committed adultery with her in his heart."

CHAPTER THREE

MARKETPLACE AND MONEY

The kingdom is a place of rest. Jesus promised rest to those who came to Him. Unlike the cultural aspirations of society that feels the need to push its way to the top, kingdom success is obtained from a place of rest. If we adopt the model of society's eclecticism, we will be on an incessant wheel of chance, a game of luck, and face the demands of the evil taskmaster mammon.

- Isaiah 32- My people will live in peaceful dwelling places, in secure homes, in undisturbed places of rest.

When we come to Christ we enter into rest. This is a place of spiritual rest. It is also a place of delight and provision. This was the promise of God to His people—peaceable habitation and quiet resting places. This is the opposite of turmoil and worry. The father commands us to enter into His rest, meaning that we must cease from human striving.

There is so much that needs to be defined here to further explain this concept of dominion and rest. The contrast between putting our hand to the plow, working while it is day; must be from the finished work of the cross and not the sweat of our brow. This revelation is obtained through sonship and not just religious activities. The kingdom exists solely through the means of hierarchical kings and sons functioning generationally to fill the earth.

The inward rulership of Christ allows us to enter into Christ Himself as our resting place. Christ is our peaceable habitation. The rule of Christ, the good shepherd, gives us rest. Striving, turmoil, confusion and undisciplined actions are the marks spiritual bastards, vagabonds and hirelings masquerading as legitimate sons. Since we have been translated into sonship, these are all a part of our past, we must cultivate a personal culture of responsible wealth building and marketplace integrity.

So how do we grow and succeed in the marketplace? I want to examine three key concepts for marketplace growth which are stewardship, scalability, and viability. In terms of business or marketplace economics two words that you will need to use in measuring how to function are scalability and viability. We will clearly define them next so you can determine how these can assist your apostolic marketplace endeavors.

Stewardship-

Stewardship is an ethic that embodies the responsible planning and management of resources. The concepts of stewardship can be applied to the environment and nature, economics, health, property, information, theology, cultural resources etc.

> *"steward," means literally*
> *"man over the house."*

Apostleship always has the function of stewardship especially in the case of Elohim's' economics, mysteries and inheritances.

We understand that stewardship is beyond just watching over and giving back what was entrusted to us but the multiplication of the goods into the lives of others.

Scalability-

- Definition- is the property of a system to handle a growing amount of work by adding resources to the system.

Scalability can be measured over multiple dimensions, such as:

- *Administrative scalability*: The ability for an increasing number of organizations or users to access a system.[iii]
- *Functional scalability*: The ability to enhance the system by adding new functionality without disrupting existing activities.

- *Geographic scalability*: The ability to maintain effectiveness during expansion from a local area to a larger region.
- *Load scalability*: The ability for a distributed system to expand and contract to accommodate heavier or lighter loads, including, the ease with which a system or component can be modified, added, or removed, to accommodate changing loads.
- *Generation scalability*: The ability of a system to scale by adopting new generations of components.
- *Heterogeneous scalability* is the ability to adopt components from different vendors.

Viability-

- Definition- when we use the term in biology, it means that it is capable of living, surviving, or thriving, especially under certain conditions.

We use the term for anything or any situation which can continue developing, growing, or living successfully. The term first emerged in the English language in 1828. It came from the French word 'Viable,' which means *"capable of life."*

Once our endeavors are scalable, and viable we must make sure they grow and multiply. Our endeavors must be capable of life for growth.

Kingdom Finances/Money

Jesus became A Curse- To liberate His Church. When God says, "I want to prosper you - what is the purpose of that wealth?

1. To establish the covenant.
2. Finance the kingdom.
3. To leave a legacy to your children.

While writing I asked a question: "God! How do you prosper your people?" He says, "Wealth comes to their hearts! "Life: The Lord says: "There are many

ways! "With an idea! Okay I get it a creative idea!-
Apostle G Maldonado, King Jesus Ministry

So, God manifests His wealth to you with a creative idea. To get those concepts, you must have a receiving spirit to get those ideas. The world today is getting ideas in different places - but original ideas are hard to come by.

Money Principle #1-

Some Things Are Worth Investing In "The kingdom of heaven is like treasure hidden in a field, which a man found and covered up. Then in his joy he goes and sells all that he has and buys that field

- Matthew 13:44–46- "Again, the kingdom of heaven is like a merchant in search of fine pearls, who, on finding one pearl of great value, went and sold all that he had and bought it."

There are so many times that Jesus uses money as a way to communicate a spiritual truth. Here his point is obvious that God's kingdom is valuable enough that a wise person would liquidate everything in order to have it.

Money Principle #2-

Wisdom And Money Provide Security For the protection of wisdom is like the protection of money. [iv]

Money Principle #3-

Prosperity Can Be a Blessing the Lord will open to you his good treasury, the heavens, to give the rain to your land in its season and to bless all the work of your hands. And you shall lend to many nations, but you shall not borrow.

- Deuteronomy 28:12 -As God lays out the potential blessings for Israel's obedience, he includes this promise: "you shall lend to many nations, but you shall not borrow."

This promise comes from a time when debt was reserved for the most desperate situations and could quite literally make someone beholden to their debtor.[v] The writer of Proverbs communicates this well when he says, "the rich rules over the poor, and the borrower is the slave of the lender." (Prov. 22:7)

Money Principle #4-

Leave A Legacy A good man leaves an inheritance to his children's children,

Money Principle #5-

Give Wealth Its Proper Place He who loves money will not be satisfied with money, nor he who loves wealth with his income; this also is vanity. (Ecclesiastes 5:10)

1. These ideas can come in a dream, or in a vision. They can come to you after a prophetic word and someone will write it down and you say, "Oh my God! I never thought about this."
2. You must cultivate the idea. You must think, "Okay! How can I work this idea?"

3. Write the idea down and put it into practice. Write it and put it into practice.
4. You don't get wealth from old ideas - only new ideas. In other words, this supernatural power is so powerful. This one idea, the creative idea is enough to make you prosper. Mumm. Jesus, Jesus, Jesus! Can I hear an Amen?

When we apply these money principles and apostolic strategies, we can create viable, scalable goals that produce results.

CHAPTER FOUR
EXPLOITS AND STRATEGIES

Just as Jesus instructed his disciples, so he instructs us today via strategy/parables. Let's overview a few apostolic strategies that Jesus taught; we can implement these concepts immediately in our efforts.

- Matthew 10- "Behold, I send you out as sheep in the midst of wolves; so be shrewd as serpents and innocent as doves.

Shrewdness-

- Definition- act if being marked by clever discerning awareness and hard-headed acumen.

Apostles must deal with godly counsel, prudency, and subtlety. We must beware of men and operate covertly. "But beware of men, for they will hand you over to the courts and scourge you in their synagogues; and you will even be brought before governors and kings for My sake, as a testimony to them and to the Gentiles. (Matthew 10:17)

Apostolic / Prophetic Utterance

- Matthew 10:19- But when they hand you over, do not worry about how or what you are to say; for it will be given you in that hour what you are to say. "For it is not you who speak, but it is the Spirit of your Father who speaks in you.

Apostles must speak with sound clarity and utterance from God. They must speak up and speak out the soundness of God's kingdom.

Endurance to End-

To amad: to take one's stand, stand primitive root; to stand, in various relations (literal and figurative, intransitive and transitive) -- abide (behind), appoint, arise, cease, confirm, continue, dwell, be employed, endure, establish, leave, make, ordain, be (over), place, (be) present (self), raise up, remain, repair, + serve, set (forth, over, -tle, up), (make to, make to be at a, with-)stand (by, fast, firm, still, up), (be at a) stay (up), tarry.

- Matthew 10: 21-22- Brother will betray brother to death, and a father his child; and children will rise up against parents and cause them to be put to death. "You will be hated by all because of My name, but it is the one who has endured to the end who will be saved.

Flee/ Know When to Disappear - (stealth mode)

- Matthew 10:23- But whenever they persecute you in one city, flee to the next; for truly I say to you, you will not finish going through the cities of Israel until the Son of Man comes.

Revelation of Mysteries- Knowledge-

Apostles must know and understand what others don't perceive; (foreknowledge, insight, and proficient insight).

- Matthew 10:26- Therefore, do not fear them, for there is nothing concealed that will not be revealed or hidden that will not be known.
- Matthew 10:27- What I tell you in the darkness, speak in the light; and what you hear whispered in your ear, proclaim upon the housetops.

God Fearing and God Trusting-

- Matthew 10:28-30 Do not fear those who kill the body but are unable to kill the soul; but rather fear Him who is able to destroy both soul and body in hell. Are not two sparrows sold for a cent? And yet not one of them will fall to the ground apart from your Father. "But the very hairs of your head are all numbered. So do not fear; you are more valuable than many sparrows.

Apostolic Boldness & Declarations-

- Matthew10:32-34- "Therefore, everyone who confesses Me before men, I will also confess him before My Father who is in heaven. But whoever denies Me before men, I will also deny him before My Father who is in heaven. Do not think that I came to bring peace on the earth; I did not come to bring peace, but a sword.

Motivated By Passion and Love of Father-

- Matthew 10: 37-39- He who loves father or mother more than Me is not worthy of Me; and he who loves son or daughter more than Me is not worthy of Me. And he who does not take his cross and follow after Me is not worthy of Me. "He who has found his life will lose it, and he who has lost his life for My sake will find it.

Overcome and Handle Persecution-

- KNOW ITS NOT PERSONAL-----IT'S AGAINST GOD'S CHURCH/KINGDOM
- SINCE WE CARRY THE KINGDOM, IT BECOMES OUR JOB TO FIGHT BACK

Persecution Against the Church

- Acts 8:1-3, Saul was in hearty agreement with putting him to death and on that day a great persecution began against the church in Jerusalem, and they were all scattered throughout the regions of Judea and Samaria, except the apostles. Some devout men buried Stephen and made loud lamentation over him. But Saul began ravaging the church, entering house after house, and dragging off men and women, he would put them in prison.

Spiritual Warfare-

We must use offensive warfare, spiritual tactics as well as defensive.

- offensive tactics

- defensive tactic
- group tactic
- protective tactic
- strategy/recovery

We need systematic approaches to perform apostolic movements. We must practice intentional warfare strategies.

Tipping Point –

"The point at which the momentum for change becomes unstoppable." – Gladwell

Apostolically and Prophetically, I believe we are reaching this point now!

CHAPTER FIVE
TANGIBLE RESULTS

This chapter will be a detailed case study to explain the momentum apostolic theory that creates results. If we look at a pattern in the bible life of Moses and Solomon we see great results came from prudence and posterity. When Moses starts out, he only was desiring to see one slave set free, however as he spends time growing his ability to manage the (weight of glory) from God.

He becomes a changed man; he enters a season of divine acceleration. This momentum takes him from the backside of the desert into becoming one of the greatest apostolic leaders of bible history. Moses was truly apostolic in nature since he was sent out on a mission from God Himself to recapture lost citizens of the kingdom. His prophetic gifting did not remove him of Apostleship and the assignment of restoration. The four main attributes that make him truly apostolic in nature were pioneering, exploiting, miraculous power displayed and lastly the responsibility and charge to manage the outcome.

When we look at the functioning of the Prophets which seem similar, they did not have the burden from God to ensure the release from captivity, they spoke of it but did not birth or establish the results. Apostleship is about getting results for the Father, not just carrying the burden, seeing it, or overseeing the people. The apostleship is like a general contractor that has to ensure all components are completed and the finished project can pass examination by outside entities.

The bible says that Moses was given charge over his people in Hebrews, just like Jesus was given charge over God's inheritance.

- Hebrews 3:2- For he was faithful to God, who appointed him, just as Moses served faithfully when he was entrusted with God's entire[c] house.

This is so important if we shall see efficacy and tangible results in our ministry exploits. So, let's continue our study of Moses' life. The bible says this about Moses in Exodus.

- Exodus 4:18- So Moses went back home to Jethro, his father-in-law. "Please let me return to my relatives in Egypt," Moses said. "I don't even know if they are still alive."

Moses after running from Egypt is in the land with Jethro is father-in-law and although He is called, he gets counsel from Jethro. Counsel is one of the distinct ingredients to his results of ministry. This is an early peek into the meekness that makes Moses one of the most useful and productive people of the bible. Meekness is the quality of power or authority under restraint for the purpose of diplomacy and prudency.

Why Moses sought counsel, is the same reason you Apostle, will need to seek counsel. Many are the plans of a man, but the Lord will establish them and direct his steps. This direction cannot be taken lightly if you and I will get results from heaven to earth.

Gods' direction, great decisions and avoiding distractions will assist you in maintaining what God is establishing in our lives. I have seen many a prophet and apostle miss the mark in this area. This is why God had to perform a great work in Moses in the desert, on the backside of glory and in obscurity. For Moses to manage the assignment or charge of God's people it took a dexterity that comes only with temperance and being under the order of God. In the wilderness God ordered Moses' life, actions, thoughts, and temperament.

Receiving Counsel is a Skill-

Notice Moses did not have twenty counselors or voices speaking to him, but the one that was placed clearly in his path. He was not the most spiritual, but He was the most available for God's inclination and wisdom. Note that God can use even seemingly ungodly or unseasoned prophets to declare a truth to us, even though we are Apostles. Failure to receive from God's counsel will bring negative results and eventual demise. Moses did NOT need Jethro to give Him the word of the Lord, but directions and wisdom on how to manage them as a man. It was not very deep spiritual insights he was obtaining from Jethro, but balancing the assignment with his manhood and human limitations.

Second key component I see in Moses' life was his tenacity and pursuit despite the odds.

- Exodus 5:1-2– Moses and Aaron go to the Pharaoh to tell him that the LORD God of Israel commanded that the Hebrews should be free to go with Moses into the wilderness. The Pharaoh refused to let the Hebrew people go.

We all know the story it was a continual refusal of Pharaoh to what God had spoken, and plagues followed his disobedience. Regardless of how many times it would take Moses, he was committed to seeing the process through. We must have this same tenacity because pioneering is just the beginning, holding the charge is the ultimate test of character. If we are only excited at the genesis of a project but do not remain consistent, we will not see results we desire.

All apostolic accomplishments have their own degree of resistance and toiling to see results. Even small drops of water can create great depths of change if they are consistent enough over time. So, Apostle, we must be in for the long haul. How about eighty years or an entire lifetime building to see the results that will last.

Building With Proven Results Takes Tenacity-

Third key to Moses results was his ability to hear God and move in faith.

- Exodus 14- Then the LORD gave these instructions to Moses:[2] "Order the Israelites to turn back and camp by Pi-hahiroth between Migdol and the sea. Camp there along the shore, across from Baal-zephon. I have planned this in order

> to display my glory through Pharaoh and his whole army.

Moses was given direct instructions from God at every endeavor to get the predetermined results that only God could accomplish. This is where we are tasked to be the most humble, submissive and directable. Moses' temperament was the key factor in the people following the orders of God as spoken by Moses. He, like all great apostolic leaders, did not move without orders from God. The bible says orders for a reason because they were non-negotiable. We see the contrast with King Saul who decided to go against God's orders and his demise was the result. Moses received instructions, but he ordered the people. Apostles must order people to obey what God Himself has planned.

The word ORDER- דבר (*D.B.R*) is commonly found in the Biblical text and means to "speak," as in the phrase *vayiDaBeR YHWH el moshe l'mor* (and YHWH spoke to Moses saying). The ancient Hebrew understanding of "speaking," or a "speech," is an ordered arrangement of words, so the verb דבר (*D.B.R*) may better be translated as "order," as in "And YHWH gave orders to Moses saying."

A commanding officer does not "speak" to his troops; instead, he formulates his action plans and determined the best means to have these plans conducted. Once all of this is determined, he gives his "orders," an ordered arrangement of ideas."

So, ordering is different from demanding from people but more so the concept of giving clear plans that will result in the peace and order of God.

I have found that environments or ministries that lack peace are usually due to lack of ordered plans or completion of directives. This we know is one of the greatest components that distinguishes Apostleship from the pastoral grace in the kingdom.

Many today speak about order or governing as Apostles but without true understanding of what the root of the words mean we can still move in chaos or confusion.

Or-Der

Order- Another noun derived from the root דבר (*D.B.R*) is the word דברה (*devorah*, Strong's #1682), which means "bee." A beehive is a colony of insects that live in a perfectly ordered society.

The word דברה (*devorah*) is also the personal name *Deborah* (Strong's #1683), which of course means "bee."

Another common word derived from the root דבר (*D.B.R*) is מדבר (*mid'bar*, Strong's #4057) meaning a "wilderness." In the ancient Hebrew mind the wilderness, in contrast to the cities, is a place of order. Many people today live in the cities, a place of high crime and a place of hurrying, rushing, and busying oneself with all day-to-day tasks. The city can easily be seen as a place of chaos.

The four main attributes that make him truly apostolic in nature were pioneering, exploiting, miraculous power displayed and lastly the responsibility and charge to manage the outcome. Results are ordered once we fulfill the necessary inputs, just like in a mathematical equation the results are ordered. Results are the exact derivative of the correct ordered steps taken. The great news about this concept is once we follow the instructions the results are guaranteed and there is no failure in God's directions.

Lastly, we see from Moses' life was stamped with many encounters with God that allowed him to carry the glory. The glory is the realm of results of the Kingdom. Encountering the Glory of God is necessary to get supernatural results from God.

"Now therefore, I pray, if I have found grace in Your sight, show me now Your way, that I may know You and that I may find grace in Your sight. And consider that this nation is Your people. "And He said, "My Presence will go with you, and I will give you rest." [18] And he said, "Please, show me Your glory." And the LORD said, "Here is a place by Me, and you shall stand on the rock. [22] So it shall be, while My glory passes by, that I will put you in the cleft of the rock and will cover you with My hand while I pass by. [23] Then I will take away My hand, and you shall see My back; but My face shall not be seen." (Exodus 33:12-23)

How else can we see results but with the presence, rest, and grace of God? The grace allows for our human fragility and covers the hidden parts of our flesh. Just like in this passage that God showed Moses his backside while covering him in the cleft of the rock. This grace of God covers our human weakness in the demonstration of power administered via God's love for us.

Apostolic grace is a tangible commodity of the kingdom, and we can harness it for kingdom endeavors.

The glory of God is also synonymous with God's dunamis power because it is ad place of total dependency on Elohim.

This place of glory has no need for human striving or human aid. It is dependent on the God quality of loving kindness to accomplish the will of the father. Now the glory of God or shekinah is such a notable topic for exploration that I will leave that for another book, at a later date, but know it's the tangibility factor within the earth. The glory of God is not an experience but an actual quark or entity that carries the nature of God himself. When we encounter the glory, we understand the beauty and delight of God.

CHAPTER SIX
UNDERSTANDING YOUR REIGN

The LORD reigns, let the earth be glad; let the distant shores rejoice. Clouds and thick darkness surround him; righteousness and justice are the foundation of his throne. Fire goes before him and consumes his foes on every side. (Psalm 97)

In the New Testament we see Jesus explain the purpose or the rules of engaging in his sovereign reign as an appointed officer. "I am the vine; you are the branches. If you remain in me and I in you, you will bear much fruit; apart from me you can do nothing. This is to my Father's glory, that you bear much fruit, showing yourselves to be my disciples. (John. 15:5,8)

It is for the glory of my Father Jesus says that we bear fruit or produce in every sphere of influence. This is however only possible within the vine or offspring of

Christ rulership. Sonship is the bridge between visions and tangible results and productivity.

Sonship makes us accountable, faithful servants in our father's house (kingdom). We must go up by means of adoption to bear fruit that is not devoured by the enemy.

Moses was a prophet to the people, but an Apostle to God.

Psalms 99:6, which says plainly, "Moses and Aaron were among his priests. The bible continually speaks of our appointment in terms of faithfulness to God and having the charge over a house. This is what our rulership and the tenure of it collide for purpose sake. For he was faithful to God, who appointed him, just as Moses served faithfully when he was entrusted with God's entire house.

Hebrews starts with stating that our priest and Apostle was Christ himself, and then compares Him to Moses, also a priest and Apostle.

John Lierman, a great Jewish scholar also concludes Moses as priest and Apostle in his book with great depth of clarity and research.

Hebrews 3 says, But Christ, as the Son, is in charge of God's entire house. And we are God's house, if we keep our courage and remain confident in our hope in Christ

Reign-
- the period during which a sovereign rule.

Thrones-
- seat of honour, throne
- the state of being a ruler: [vi]
- Elizabeth II ascended/came to the throne (= became queen of Britain) when her father died.
- Queen Victoria was on the throne (= was queen) at that time.

A throne is your apostolic authority or place where your rulership extends from. In the marketplace it would be the assigned spheres of influence that God has ordained for His purposes.

This cannot be manipulated or orchestrated by the hands of man for the bible says that God sets all men in authority. Authority in this sense is our authorized place of influence and rulership. One cannot come to power (dominion) in any arena of industries without having a throne or seat of influence. We understand that man must labor in his efforts to accomplish God's will but there is still a sovereign decision of the level of altitude pre-determined by God's will.

Dominion is beyond just financial influence and accumulation of status within society. It is the occupancy and right or tenure to remain in position indefinitely. God said to David he made an everlasting covenant with him to set up his throne until Christ reigned.

Kingship

- The domain ruled by a king, a kingdom. A monarchy, The position, rank, dignity, or dominion

>of a king. The period or tenure of a king; a reign.

The idea of kingship from the first was that of a ruler representing God. It was only after a bitter experience that the kingship was no longer regarded as a divine gift, and traditions have been revised to illustrate the opposition to secular authority.[vii]

CHAPTER SEVEN
MANAGEMENT

Proper management of resources like time and finances is indicative of maintained momentum. At times, we hurry through processes, fail to implement systems and the result can be chaotic. What we fail to steward, becomes unruly, unproductive, and bothersome, and a thorn in our flesh. These kinds of thorns are just what Paul spoke of, for they buffet us back into places of mediocrity and depravity. They cause us to shrink back for million-dollar proposals, opportunities of advancement and promotion. A steward is a manager. "And the Lord said, Who then is that faithful and wise STEWARD, whom his lord shall make ruler over his household, to give them their portion of meat in due season? Blessed is that servant, whom his lord when he cometh shall find so doing. (Luke 12:42). We can claim ownership and ultimate authority over nothing. Secondly, we were created to be God's image-bearers. As image-bearers we have been given a commission to have dominion over God's creation. This is a call to stewardship, not self-interested exploitation. We are called to be conformed to the image of God to others and to the rest of the nonhuman creation. As Christ is the fullest expression of the image of God, our model for dominion is that of self-sacrificing servant. The stewardship model acknowledges that God is the Creator, Preserver, and Owner of everything. "The biblical truth—that it all belongs to God.

- Deuteronomy 8:11-20 - [11] Be careful that you do not forget the Lord your God, failing to observe his commands, his laws and his decrees that I am giving you this day. [12] Otherwise, when you eat and are satisfied, when you build fine houses and settle down, [13] and when your herds and flocks grow large and your silver and gold increase and all you have is multiplied, [14] then your heart will become proud and you will forget the Lord your God, who brought you out of Egypt, out of the land of slavery. [15] He led you through the vast and dreadful wilderness, that thirsty and waterless land, with its venomous snakes and scorpions. He brought you water out of hard rock. [16] He gave you manna to eat in the wilderness, something your ancestors had never known, to humble and test you so that in the end it might go well with you. [17] You may say to yourself, "My power and the strength of my hands have produced this wealth for me." [18] But remember the Lord your God, for it is he who gives you the ability to produce wealth, and so confirms his covenant, which he swore to your ancestors, as it is today. [19] If you ever forget the Lord your God and follow other gods and worship and bow down to them, I testify against you today that you will surely be destroyed. [20] Like the nations the Lord destroyed before you, so you will be destroyed for not obeying the Lord your God.

Emotions, Ambitions, Perspectives-

We must manage these hidden areas of our lives to keep the holy spirits accessible to us for breakthrough. Inward government is necessary for outward success. Managing our emotions is not just the work of the Holy Spirit for we are called to self-governance. Self-mastery ("soberly" in NKJV) is self-government or self-control, the foundation of a strong godly life, growth, and producing [viii]fruit. If a person cannot govern himself, if he cannot master his passions, he will certainly not have a good relationship with his fellow man or God. His life will be marked by major excesses.

- 2 Corinthians 5:9- And for this reason also we make it our ambition, whether at home or in exile, to please Him perfectly.

Ambition-

Our ambition must be grounded within the boundaries of God. Ambition is defined as "an intense drive for success or power; a desire to achieve honor, wealth or fame." To be ambitious, in the worldly sense, is to be determined to have more than your neighbor. [ix]Its motto is "he with the most toys wins;" ambition strives to be number one. However, in the Bible, the word ambition takes on a whole new dimension: "Make it your ambition to lead a quiet life, to mind your own business and to work with your hands …"(1 Thessalonians 4:11; cf. Philippians 1:17; Ephesians 5:8-10).

Perspective-

Perspective- has a Latin root meaning "look through" or "perceive," and all the meanings of *perspective* have something to do with looking. If you observe the world from a dog's perspective, you see through the dog's eyes.   This is the lens by which we see life

CHAPTER EIGHT
MOUNTAINS AND MOVEMENT

The Mountain of The House of The Lord-

This is the message that was revealed to Isaiah, son of Amoz concerning Judah and Jerusalem.

In the last days the mountain of the house of the LORD will be established as the chief of the mountains; it will be raised above the hills, and all nations will stream to it. And many people will come and say; "Come, let us go up to the mountain of the LORD, to the house of the God of Jacob. He will teach us His ways so that we may walk in His paths." For the law will go forth from Zion, and the word of the LORD from Jerusalem.

Apostles must climb the mountain of the Lord, not just prophesy, and plant churches. They must have a higher vantage point of view, in order to create massive endeavors. Momentum can directly be related to the height at which they scale the mountain of the Lord, for the descent causes us to gain momentum. Paul's encounters with Jesus I believe is what jump started his ministry and propelled him forward. His momentum was tangible to all the churches.

We can expect all sorts of adventures during our apostolic call. These occurrences do not disqualify us but are evidence of the kingdom calling.

- Witchcraft attacks/animal attacks/people attacks
- Confrontations with sorcery
- People leaving our ministry/betrayal
- People getting offended by Paul's ministry/teaching
- Being misunderstood
- Being called alone and apart
- Laid hands on by prophets/elders to conform our assignment from God

- Holy Spirit bearing witness of our personal call to other leaders

The Call –

- Acts 13:1-3 - Now there were in the church that was at Antioch certain prophets and teachers; as Barnabas, and Simeon that was called Niger, and Lucius of Cyrene, and Manaen, which had been brought up with Herod the tetrarch, and Saul. As they ministered to the Lord, and fasted, the Holy Ghost said, separate me Barnabas and Saul for the work whereunto I have called them. And when they had fasted and prayed, and laid their hands on them, they sent them away.

Events of Paul's Missions-

Sail to Cyprus - Preach the Gospel

- Acts 13:4-5- So they, being sent forth by the Holy Ghost, departed unto Seleucia; and from thence they sailed to Cyprus. And when they were at Salamis, they preached the word of God in the synagogues of the Jews: and they had also John to their minister.

QUESTIONNAIRE

&

PRACTICAL TIPS

What was your apostolic call like?

An Encounter with a False Prophet

- Acts 6-12- And when they had gone through the isle unto Paphos, they found a certain sorcerer, a false prophet, a Jew, whose name was Barjesus: Which was with the deputy of the country, Sergius Paulus, a prudent man, who called for Barnabas and Saul, and desired to hear the word of God. But Elymas the sorcerer (for so is his name by interpretation) withstood them, seeking to turn away the deputy from the faith.

What encounters with resistance in business/ministry have you experienced and what did you learn from them?

- Then Saul, (Paul,) filled with the Holy Ghost, set his eyes on him, And said, O full of all subtilty and all mischief, thou child of the devil, thou enemy of all righteousness, wilt thou not cease to pervert the right ways of the Lord? And now, behold, the hand of the Lord is upon thee, and thou shalt be blind, not seeing the sun for a season. And immediately there fell on him a mist and a darkness; and he went about seeking some to lead him by the hand. Then the deputy, when he saw what was done, believed, being astonished at the doctrine of the Lord.

What can you learn from Paul's Apostolic Boldness?

John quits and returns home

- Acts 13:13- Now when Paul and his company loosed from Paphos, they came to Perga in

Pamphylia: and John departing from them returned to Jerusalem.

Paul was confronted by evil men- & speculation and contention about Paul

- But the unbelieving Jews stirred up the Gentiles, and made their minds evil affected against the brethren. Long time therefore abode they are speaking boldly in the Lord, which gave testimony unto the word of his grace, and granted signs and wonders to be done by their hands. But the multitude of the city was divided: and part held with the Jews, and part with the apostles.

How have and will you handle betrayal and personal accusations about your Apostleship or Business?

Paul's life was threatened- although he was speaking the truth

- And when there was an assault made both of the Gentiles, and also of the Jews with their rulers, to use them despitefully, and to stone them,

Traveling to Comfort Churches/Ministers/Strengthened the local church

- Confirming the souls of the disciples, and exhorting them to continue in the faith, and that we must through much tribulation enter into the kingdom of God. And when they had ordained them elders in every church, and had prayed with fasting, they commended them to the Lord, on whom they believed. And there they abode long time with the disciples.

What regions are you called to?

Have you planted in other regions beyond your local works?

Have you created a system to franchise/duplicate your ministry/business model?

Apostles did many acts for the local church
- Confirmed the disciples who they had led to the Lord
- Exhorted them
- Ordained Elders in the churches which had been established
- Preached at Perga
- Sailed back to Antioch from where their journey began
- Assembled with the church there and gave testimony concerning all that God had done.

What's your ministry/business succession process?

Do you have a protégé?

Do you have interns or mentees?

- List their names and your assignment to them

Paul debates doctrine

The Debate at Jerusalem

- Acts 1-6 And certain men which came down from Judaea taught the brethren, and said, except ye be circumcised after the manner of Moses, ye cannot be saved. When therefore Paul and Barnabas had no small dissension and disputation with them, they determined that Paul and Barnabas, and certain other of them, should go up to Jerusalem unto the apostles and elders about this question.

What doctrine are you called to defend, debunk or expose to the body of Christ?

- But there rose up certain of the sect of the Pharisees which believed, saying, That it was needful to circumcise them, and to command them to keep the law of Moses.

Do you have an apostolic council (other apostles that you consort for direction)?

Paul Rebukes and corrects other leaders

Paul rebukes Peter

- Galatians 2:11-21   Vs.11-13   But when Peter was come to Antioch, I withstood him to the face, because he was to be blamed. 12. For before that certain came from James, he did eat with the Gentiles: but when they were come, he withdrew and separated himself, fearing them which were of the circumcision.
- And the other Jews dissembled likewise with him; insomuch that Barnabas also was carried away with their dissimulation.

Are you called to correct doctrine, or other leaders? If so, how do you know?

- The Next section covers Paul's doctrines in details. Can you share your thoughts or understanding on each topic? Please read each topic and meditate on this Apostolic model. Are you following biblical apostolic doctrine or tradition of men? How can you use these doctrines to influence marketplace reformation?

Paul's Epistles-

Of the 27 books of the New Testament, the Holy Spirit used Apostle Paul to write 13. Some scholars believe that Paul also wrote the book of Hebrews

ROMANS

- Theme: Righteousness of God

- Paul's epistle to the Christians at Rome, speaks of Gods provision of Righteousness, based on faith in Jesus Christ, apart from works.

1 CORINTHIANS

- Theme: Christian Conduct
- In this epistle Paul addresses issues such as: division, immorality, carnality, Christian marriage, Christian liberty, the Lords Supper, spiritual gifts, the resurrection, and general instructions.

2 CORINTHIANS

- Theme: Paul's Authority
- In the second epistle to the Corinthians Paul defends his Apostleship by giving an account of his service to God, shown by his sufferings and all the persecutions he endured.

GALATIANS

- Theme: Salvation by Grace
- In this epistle to the Galatian Churches, Paul has to deal with the false teachings that had

spread through the churches by certain individuals who said that: While salvation was of Christ, works were also necessary. These kinds of teachings were causing people to depart from trusting Christ and turning to keep the law, for salvation. Paul uses the example of Abraham, and how he was justified by faith alone, 430 years before the Mosaic Law.

EPHESIANS

- Theme: In Christ
- This epistle to the Ephesians speaks of the Christians exalted position in Christ and the living out of that position in our everyday lives. Also addressed, is how the division between Jew and Gentile has been broken down and that in Christ we are one body.

PHILIPPIANS

- Theme: Rejoicing in the Lord
- Paul wrote this epistle while in prison at Rome. In the mist of personal hardship and sacrifice

Paul writes this epistle to the Philippians Christians; displaying the joy of the Lord, which sustained him

COLOSSIANS

- Theme: Christ's Preeminence
- This epistle was written because of false teachings that had been brought into the church, which assigned to Christ a position under the Godhead instead of being a part. The teachings included the exaltation of angels, as well as an infatuation with them. In this epistle, Paul shows the superiority of Christ as Lord and places Him as head of the church.

1 THESSALONIANS

- Theme: The Christian's hope
- Paul had sent Timothy to the church at Thessalonica to find out how they were doing; this epistle was written after Timothy returned with a good report of the faith and love that they had for Apostle Paul. One of the highlights of this

epistle is found in 4:13-18, which speaks of the return of Christ for His people, the Christian's blessed hope.

2 THESSALONIANS

- Theme: The Day of the Lord
- This epistle was written to ease the troubled minds of the Christians at Thessalonica; that the tribulations that they were experiencing were not the day of the Lord in which, God would pour out His wrath upon this earth, in judgment of all the ungodly. Paul reminds them of what he had taught them concerning the man of sin, how that he would be revealed before that day.

1 TIMOTHY

- Theme: Church order
- The purpose of this epistle to Timothy was for personal instruction as a good minister of Jesus Christ; also instructions concerning church order. A key verse is found in 3:15, which states, " ..that thou mayest know how thou oughtest to

conduct thyself in the house of God , which is the pillar and ground of the truth."

2 TIMOTHY

- Theme: Be a Faithful Servant
- The 2nd. epistle of Paul to Timothy was written while in prison awaiting his execution and may have been his last epistle. Abandoned by most of his friends (1:15, 4:16) Paul speaks of the time of his departure as being at hand (4:6). Paul admonishes Timothy to endure hardness as a good soldier of the Lord and preach the word of God.

TITUS

- Theme: Setting the Church in Order
- This epistle to Titus was instructions for him to ordain elders, the qualifications and duties of elders, as well as exhortations to godly living.

PHILEMON

- Theme: Brotherly Love

- This epistle is a personal letter to Philemon who had an unprofitable servant named Onesimus, who after (in all probability) stole from him, ran away. Under Paul's ministry, Onesimus was converted and now Paul writes to Philemon to receive him back not only as a servant, but a brother in Christ.

Lastly, we will look at types of miracles Paul performed; Can you list the miracles that you have released in your ministry?

Paul's Miracles in order
- Peter healed the lame man at the Temple (3:7-11).
- God answered Peter in a miraculous earthquake (4:31).
- Ananias and Sapphira were slain by the Lord (5:5-10).

- Signs and wonders continued to be done by the apostles (5:12).
- Peter healed many from various cities (5:12-16).
- The prison doors were opened by an angel (5:19).
- Stephen wrought great wonders and signs (6:8).
- In Samaria, Philip did great miracles and signs (8:6,7,13).
- The Lord appeared to Saul, but Saul is unsaved until he responds to the preaching of the gospel by Ananias (9:3-9).
- Ananias healed Saul's blindness (9:17-18).
- Peter healed Aeneas (9:32-35).
- In Joppa, Peter raised Dorcus from the dead (9:39-42).
- Cornelius saw an angel. He and his family spoke in tongues, but he was saved by responding to the preaching of the gospel by Peter (10:4,46; cf. v. 48; 11:14).

- Peter saw the vision on the roof and spoke with the Lord (10:9-22).
- A prison gate was miraculously opened (12:10).
- Paul blinded Elymus (13:11-12).
- Paul performed miracles in Iconium (14:3,4).
- At Lystra, Paul healed a crippled man (14:8-18).
- Paul healed a woman possessed by an evil spirit (16:18).
- The miraculous earthquake unloosed all the chains and doors in the Philippian prison (16:26).
- In Ephesus, twelve men spoke in tongues, and prophesied (19:6).
- Paul performed other miracles in Ephesus (19:11,12).
- In Troas, Paul raised Eutychus from the dead (20:8-12).

- Paul was not affected by the viper at Melita (28:3-6). He also healed those on the island who were diseased (28:8-9).

What did you learn about your own apostolic journey from reading Paul's account in detail?

- *Which miracles are you believing God to use for you to minister?*

- *Which are currently present in your ministry?*

- *What are the similarities?*

- *What is God speaking about your reach now?*

- *Mandate?*

- *What sphere of influence are you currently operating in?*

- *Finance?*

- *Religion?*

- *Family?*

- *Government/Politics?*

- *Media?*

- *How is your mandate going to change people's lives?*

- *How will it affect their economics, relationships?*

- *What areas do you see momentum in your life/business?*

- *How will you use the momentum of now to thrust you into your next success?*

- *Who shares the momentum you have or passion for your vision with you?*

- *Have you started training a team for the next level of your reach?*

Notes

Notes

For bookings, bookings, and more updates

from

Dr. Frederick Acklin

please visit:

www.Dr.FrederickAcklin.com

www.ingramcontent.com/pod-product-compliance
Lightning Source LLC
Chambersburg PA
CBHW070942080526
44589CB00013B/1608